The Practice of the Presence of God

In Modern English

Brother Lawrence

CONVERSATIONS

Introduction: At the time of de Beaufort's interviews, Brother Lawrence was in his late fifties. Joseph de Beaufort later commented that the crippled brother, who was then in charge of the upkeep of over one hundred pairs of sandals, was "rough in appearance but gentle in grace".

First Conversation: The first time I saw Brother Lawrence was upon the 3rd of August, 1666. He told me that God had done him a singular favor in his conversion at the age of eighteen. During that winter, upon seeing a tree stripped of its leaves and considering that within a little time the leaves would be renewed and after that the flowers and fruit appear, Brother Lawrence received a high view of the Providence and Power of God which has never since been effaced from his soul. This view had perfectly set him loose from the world and kindled in him such a love for God, that he could not tell whether it had increased in the forty years that he had lived since.

Brother Lawrence said he had been footman to M. Fieubert, the treasurer, and that he was a great awkward fellow who broke everything. He finally decided to enter a monastery thinking that he would there be made to smart for his awkwardness and the faults he would commit, and so he would sacrifice his life with its pleasures to God. But Brother Lawrence said that God had surprised him because he met with nothing but satisfaction in that state.

Brother Lawrence related that we should establish ourselves in a sense of God's Presence by continually conversing with Him. It was a shameful thing to quit His conversation to think of trifles and fooleries. We should feed and nourish our souls with high notions of God which would yield us great joy in being devoted to Him.

He said we ought to quicken and enliven our faith. It was lamentable we had so little. Instead of taking faith for the rule of their conduct, men amused themselves with trivial devotions which changed daily. He said that faith was sufficient to bring us to a high degree of perfection. We ought to give ourselves up to God with regard both to things temporal and spiritual and seek our satisfaction only in the fulfilling of His will. Whether God led us by suffering or by consolation all would be equal to a soul truly resigned.

He said we need fidelity in those disruptions in the ebb and flow of prayer when God tries our love to Him. This was the time for a complete act of resignation, whereof one act alone could greatly promote our spiritual advancement.

He said that as far as the miseries and sins he heard of daily in the world, he was so far from wondering at them, that, on the contrary, he was surprised there were not more considering the malice sinners were capable of. For his part, he prayed for them. But knowing that God could remedy the mischief they did when He pleased, he gave himself no further trouble.

Brother Lawrence said to arrive at such resignation as God requires, we should carefully watch over all the passions that mingle in spiritual as well as temporal things. God would give light concerning those passions to those who truly desire to serve Him.

At the end of this first conversation Brother Lawrence said that if my purpose for the visit was to sincerely discuss how to serve God, I might come to him as often as I pleased and without any fear of being troublesome. If this was not the case, then I ought visit him no more.

Second Conversation: Brother Lawrence told me he had always been governed by love without selfish views. Since he resolved to make the love of God the end of all his actions, he had found reasons to be well satisfied with his method. He was pleased when he could take up a straw from the ground for the love of God, seeking Him only, and nothing else, not even His gifts.

He said he had been long troubled in mind from a certain belief that he should be damned. All the men in the world could not have persuaded him to the contrary. This trouble of mind had lasted four years during which time he had suffered much.

Finally he reasoned: I did not engage in a religious life but for the love of God. I have endeavored to act only for Him. Whatever becomes of me, whether I be lost or saved, I will always continue to act purely for the love of God. I shall have this good at least that till death I shall have done all that is in me to love Him. From that time on Brother Lawrence lived his life in perfect liberty and continual joy. He placed his sins between himself and God to tell Him that he did not deserve His favors yet God still continued to bestow them in abundance.

Brother Lawrence said that in order to form a habit of conversing with God continually and referring all we do to Him, we must at first apply to Him with some diligence. Then, after a little care, we would find His love inwardly excite us to it without any difficulty.

He expected after the pleasant days God had given him, he would have his turn of pain and suffering. Yet he was not uneasy about it. Knowing that, since he could do nothing of himself, God would not fail to give him the strength to bear them.

When an occasion of practicing some virtue was offered, he addressed himself to God saying, "Lord, I cannot do this unless Thou enablest me". And then he received strength more than sufficient. When he had failed in his duty, he only confessed his fault saying to God, "I shall never do otherwise, if You leave me to myself. It is You who must hinder my falling and mend what is amiss." Then, after this, he gave himself no further uneasiness about it.

Brother Lawrence said we ought to act with God in the greatest simplicity, speaking to Him frankly and plainly, and imploring His assistance in our affairs just as they happen. God never failed to grant it, as Brother Lawrence had often experienced.

He said he had been lately sent into Burgundy to buy the provision of wine for the community. This was a very unwelcome task for him because he had no turn for business and because he was lame and could not go about the boat but by rolling himself over the casks. Yet he gave himself no uneasiness about it, nor about the purchase of the wine. He said to God, it was His business he was about, and that he afterwards found it very well performed. He mentioned that it had turned out the same way the year before when he was sent to Auvergne.

So, likewise, in his business in the kitchen (to which he had naturally a great aversion), having accustomed himself to do everything there for the love of God and asking for His grace to do his work well, he had found everything easy during the fifteen years that he had been employed there. He was very pleased with the post he was now in. Yet he was as ready to quit that as the former, since he tried to please God by doing little things for the love of Him in any work he did. With him the set times of prayer were not different from other times. He retired to pray according to the directions of his superior, but he did not need such retirement nor ask for it because his greatest business did not divert him from God.

Since he knew his obligation to love God in all things, and as he endeavored to do so, he had no need of a director to advise him, but he greatly needed a confessor to absolve him. He said he was very sensible of his faults but not discouraged by them. He confessed them to God and made no excuses. Then, he peaceably resumed his usual practice of love and adoration.

In his trouble of mind, Brother Lawrence had consulted no one. Knowing only by the light of faith that God was present, he contented himself with directing all his actions to Him. He did everything with a desire to please Him and let what would come of it.

He said that useless thoughts spoil all - that the mischief began there. We ought to reject them as soon as we perceived their impertinence and return to our communion with God. In the beginning he had often passed his time appointed for prayer in rejecting wandering thoughts and falling right back into them. He could never regulate his devotion by certain methods as some do. Nevertheless, at first he had meditated for some time, but afterwards that went off in a manner that he could give no account of. Brother Lawrence emphasized that all bodily mortifications and other exercises are useless unless they serve to arrive at the union with God by love. He had well considered this. He found that the shortest way to go straight to God was by a continual exercise of love and doing all things for His sake.

He noted that there was a great difference between the acts of the intellect and those of the will. Acts of the intellect were comparatively of little value. Acts of the will were all important. Our only business was to love and delight ourselves in God. All possible kinds of mortification, if they were void of the love of God, could not efface a single sin. Instead, we ought, without anxiety, to expect the pardon of our sins from the blood of Jesus Christ only endeavoring to love Him with all our hearts. And he noted that God seemed to have granted the greatest favors to the greatest sinners as more signal monuments of His mercy.

Brother Lawrence said the greatest pains or pleasures of this world were not to be compared with what he had experienced of both kinds in a spiritual state. As a result he feared nothing, desiring only one thing of God - that he might not offend Him. He said he carried no guilt. "When I fail in my duty, I readily acknowledge it, saying, I am used to do so. I shall never do otherwise if I am left to myself. If I fail not, then I give God thanks acknowledging that it comes from Him."

Third Conversation: Brother Lawrence told me that the foundation of the spiritual life in him had been a high notion and esteem of God in faith. When he had once well established his faith he had no other care but to reject every other thought so he might perform all his actions for the love of God. He said when sometimes he had not thought of God for a good while he did not disquiet himself for it. Having acknowledged his wretchedness to God, he simply returned to Him with so much the greater trust in Him.

He said the trust we put in God honors Him much and draws down great graces. Also, that it was impossible not only that God should deceive but that He should long let a soul suffer which is perfectly resigned to Him and resolved to endure everything for His sake.

Brother Lawrence often experienced the ready succors of Divine Grace. And because of his experience of grace, when he had business to do, he did not think of it beforehand. When it was time to do it, he found in God, as in a clear mirror, all that was fit for him to do. When outward business diverted him a little from the thought of God a fresh remembrance coming from God invested his soul and so inflamed and transported him that it was difficult for him to contain himself. He said he was more united to God in his outward employments than when he left them for devotion in retirement.

Brother Lawrence said that the worst that could happen to him was to lose that sense of God which he had enjoyed so long. Yet the goodness of God assured him He would not forsake him utterly and that He would give him strength to bear whatever evil He permitted to happen to him. Brother Lawrence, therefore, said he feared nothing. He had no occasion to consult with anybody about his state. In the past, when he had attempted to do it, he had always come away more perplexed. Since Brother Lawrence was ready to lay down his life for the love of God, he had no apprehension of danger.

He said that perfect resignation to God was a sure way to heaven, a way in which we have always sufficient light for our conduct. In the beginning of the spiritual life we ought to be faithful in doing our duty and denying ourselves and then, after a time, unspeakable pleasures followed. In difficulties we need only have recourse to Jesus Christ and beg His grace with which everything became easy.

Brother Lawrence said that many do not advance in the Christian progress because they stick in penances and particular exercises while they neglect the love of God which is the end. This appeared plainly by their works and was the reason why we see so little solid virtue. He said there needed neither art nor science for going to God, but only a heart resolutely determined to apply itself to nothing but Him and to love Him only.

Fourth Conversation: Brother Lawrence spoke with great openness of heart concerning his manner of going to God whereof some part is related already. He told me that all consists in one hearty renunciation of everything which we are sensible does not lead to God. We might accustom ourselves to a continual conversation with Him with freedom and in simplicity. We need only to recognize God intimately present with us and address ourselves to Him every moment. We need to beg His assistance for knowing His will in things doubtful and for rightly performing those which we plainly see He requires of us, offering them to Him before we do them, and giving Him thanks when we have completed them.

In our conversation with God we should also engage in praising, adoring, and loving Him incessantly for His infinite goodness and perfection. Without being discouraged on account of our sins, we should pray for His grace with a perfect confidence, as relying upon the infinite merits of our Lord. Brother Lawrence said that God never failed offering us His grace at each action. It never failed except when Brother Lawrence's thoughts had wandered from a sense of God's Presence, or he forgot to ask His assistance. He said that God always gave us light in our doubts, when we had no other design but to please Him.

Our sanctification did not depend upon changing our works. Instead, it depended on doing that for God's sake which we commonly do for our own. He thought it was lamentable to see how many people mistook the means for the end, addicting themselves to certain works which they performed very imperfectly by reason of their human or selfish regards. The most excellent method he had found for going to God was that of doing our common business without any view of pleasing men but purely for the love of God.

Brother Lawrence felt it was a great delusion to think that the times of prayer ought to differ from other times. We are as strictly obliged to adhere to God by action in the time of action, as by prayer in its season. His own prayer was nothing else but a sense of the presence of God, his soul being at that time insensible to everything but Divine Love. When the appointed times of prayer were past, he found no difference, because he still continued with God, praising and blessing Him with all his might. Thus he passed his life in continual joy. Yet he hoped that God would give him somewhat to suffer when he grew stronger.

Brother Lawrence said we ought, once and for all, heartily put our whole trust in God, and make a total surrender of ourselves to Him, secure that He would not deceive us. We ought not weary of doing little things for the love of God, who regards not the greatness of the work, but the love with which it is performed. We should not wonder if, in the beginning, we often failed in our endeavors, but that at last we should gain a habit which will naturally produce its acts in us without our care and to our exceeding great delight.

The whole substance of religion was faith, hope, and charity. In the practice of these we become united to the will of God. Everything else is indifferent and to be used as a means that we may arrive at our end and then be swallowed up by faith and charity. All things are possible to him who believes. They are less difficult to him who hopes. They are more easy to him who loves, and still more easy to him who perseveres in the practice of these three virtues. The end we ought to propose to ourselves is to become, in this life, the most perfect worshippers of God we can possibly be, and as we hope to be through all eternity.

We must, from time to time, honestly consider and thoroughly examine ourselves. We will, then, realize that we are worthy of great contempt. Brother Lawrence noted that when we directly confront ourselves in this manner, we will understand why we are subject to all kinds of misery and problems. We will realize why we are subject to changes and fluctuations in our health, mental outlook, and dispositions. And we will, indeed, recognize that we deserve all the pain and labors God sends to humble us.

After this, we should not wonder that troubles, temptations, oppositions, and contradictions happen to us from men. We ought, on the contrary, to submit ourselves to them and bear them as long as God pleases as things highly advantageous to us. The greater perfection a soul aspires after, the more dependent it is upon Divine Grace.

Being questioned by one of his own community (to whom he was obliged to open himself) by what means he had attained such an habitual sense of God, Brother Lawrence told him that, since his first coming to the monastery, he had considered God as the end of all his thoughts and desires, as the mark to which they should tend, and in which they should terminate.

He noted that in the beginning of his novitiate he spent the hours appointed for private prayer in thinking of God so as to convince his mind and impress deeply upon his heart the Divine existence. He did this by devout sentiments and submission to the lights of faith, rather than by studied reasonings and elaborate meditations. By this short and sure method he exercised himself in the knowledge and love of God, resolving to use his utmost endeavor to live in a continual sense of His Presence, and, if possible, never to forget Him more.

When he had thus, in prayer, filled his mind with great sentiments of that Infinite Being, he went to his work appointed in the kitchen (for he was then cook for the community). There having first considered severally the things his office required, and when and how each thing was to be done, he spent all the intervals of his time, both before and after his work, in prayer.

When he began his business, he said to God with a filial trust in Him, "O my God, since Thou art with me, and I must now, in obedience to Thy commands, apply my mind to these outward things, I beseech Thee to grant me the grace to continue in Thy Presence; and to this end do Thou prosper me with Thy assistance. Receive all my works, and possess all my affections." As he proceeded in his work, he continued his familiar conversation with his Maker, imploring His grace, and offering to Him all his actions.

When he had finished, he examined himself how he had discharged his duty. If he found well, he returned thanks to God. If otherwise, he asked pardon and, without being discouraged, he set his mind right again. He then continued his exercise of the presence of God as if he had never deviated from it. "Thus," said he, "by rising after my falls, and by frequently renewed acts of faith and love, I am come to a state wherein it would be as difficult for me not to think of God as it was at first to accustom myself to it."

As Brother Lawrence had found such an advantage in walking in the presence of God, it was natural for him to recommend it earnestly to others. More strikingly, his example was a stronger inducement than any arguments he could propose. His very countenance was edifying with such a sweet and calm devotion appearing that he could not but affect the beholders.

It was observed, that in the greatest hurry of business in the kitchen, he still preserved his recollection and heavenly-mindedness. He was never hasty nor loitering, but did each thing in its season with an even uninterrupted composure and tranquillity of spirit. "The time of business," said he, "does not with me differ from the time of prayer.

In the noise and clutter of my kitchen, while several persons are at the same time calling for different things, I possess God in as great tranquillity as if I were upon my knees at the Blessed Supper."

LETTERS

Introduction: Brother Lawrence's letters are the very heart and soul of what is titled 'The Practice of the Presence of God'. All of these letters were written during the last ten years of his life. Many of them were to long-time friends, a Carmelite sister and a sister at a nearby convent. One or both of these friends were from his native village, perhaps relatives.

The first letter was probably written to the prioress of one of these convents. The second letter was written to Brother Lawrence's own spiritual adviser. Note that the fourth letter is written in the third person where Brother Lawrence describes his own experience. The letters follow the tradition of substituting M— for specific names.

First Letter: You so earnestly desire that I describe the method by which I arrived at that habitual sense of God's presence, which our merciful Lord has been pleased to grant me. I am complying with your request with my request that you show my letter to no one. If I knew that you would let it be seen, all the desire I have for your spiritual progress would not be enough to make me comply.

The account I can give you is: Having found in many books different methods of going to God and divers practices of the spiritual life, I thought this would serve rather to puzzle me than facilitate what I sought after, which was nothing but how to become wholly God's. This made me resolve to give the all for the All. After having given myself wholly to God, to make all the satisfaction I could for my sins, I renounced, for the love of Him, everything that was not He, and I began to live as if there was none but He and I in the world.

Sometimes I considered myself before Him as a poor criminal at the feet of his judge. At other times I beheld Him in my heart as my Father, as my God. I worshipped Him the oftenest I could, keeping my mind in His holy presence and recalling it as often as I found it wandered from Him. I made this my business, not only at the appointed times of prayer but all the time; every hour, every minute, even in the height of my work, I drove from my mind everything that interrupted my thoughts of God.

I found no small pain in this exercise. Yet I continued it, notwithstanding all the difficulties that occurred. And I tried not to trouble or disquiet myself when my mind wandered. Such has been my common practice ever since I entered religious life. Though I have done it very imperfectly, I have found great advantages by it. These, I well know, are to be imputed to the mercy and goodness of God because we can do nothing without Him; and I still less than any.

When we are faithful to keep ourselves in His holy presence, and set Him always before us, this hinders our offending Him, and doing anything that may displease Him. It also begets in us a holy freedom, and, if I may so speak, a familiarity with God, where, when we ask, He supplies the graces we need. Over time, by often repeating these acts, they become habitual, and the presence of God becomes quite natural to us.

Please give Him thanks with me, for His great goodness towards me, which I can never sufficiently express, and for the many favors He has done to so miserable a sinner as I am. May all things praise Him. Amen.

Second Letter: Not finding my manner of life described in books, although I have no problem with that, yet, for reassurance, I would appreciate your thoughts about it.

In conversation some days ago a devout person told me the spiritual life was a life of grace, which begins with servile fear, which is increased by hope of eternal life, and which is consummated by pure love; that each of these states had its different steps, by which one arrives at last at that blessed consummation.

I have not followed these methods at all. On the contrary, I instinctively felt they would discourage me. Instead, at my entrance into religious life, I took a resolution to give myself up to God as the best satisfaction I could make for my sins and, for the love of Him, to renounce all besides.

For the first years, I commonly employed myself during the time set apart for devotion with thoughts of death, judgment, hell, heaven, and my sins. Thus I continued some years applying my mind carefully the rest of the day, and even in the midst of my work, to the presence of God, whom I considered always as with me, often as in my heart.

At length I began to do the same thing during my set time of prayer, which gave me joy and consolation. This practice produced in me so high an esteem for God that faith alone was enough to assure me.

Such was my beginning. Yet I must tell you that for the first ten years I suffered a great deal. During this time I fell often, and rose again presently. It seemed to me that all creatures, reason, and God Himself were against me and faith alone for me.

The apprehension that I was not devoted to God as I wished to be, my past sins always present to my mind, and the great unmerited favors which God did me, were the source of my sufferings and feelings of unworthiness. I was sometimes troubled with thoughts that to believe I had received such favors was an effect of my imagination, which pretended to be so soon where others arrived with great difficulty. At other times I believed that it was a willful delusion and that there really was no hope for me.

Finally, I considered the prospect of spending the rest of my days in these troubles. I discovered this did not diminish the trust I had in God at all. In fact, it only served to increase my faith. It then seemed that, all at once, I found myself changed. My soul, which, until that time was in trouble, felt a profound inward peace, as if she were in her center and place of rest.

Ever since that time I walk before God simply, in faith, with humility, and with love. I apply myself diligently to do nothing and think nothing which may displease Him. I hope that when I have done what I can, He will do with me what He pleases.

As for what passes in me at present, I cannot express it. I have no pain or difficulty about my state because I have no will but that of God. I endeavor to accomplish His will in all things. And I am so resigned that I would not take up a straw from the ground against His order or from any motive but that of pure love for Him.

I have ceased all forms of devotion and set prayers except those to which my state requires. I make it my priority to persevere in His holy presence, wherein I maintain a simple attention and a fond regard for God, which I may call an actual presence of God. Or, to put it another way, it is an habitual, silent, and private conversation of the soul with God. This gives me much joy and contentment. In short, I am sure, beyond all doubt, that my soul has been with God above these past thirty years. I pass over many things that I may not be tedious to you.

Yet, I think it is appropriate to tell you how I perceive myself before God, whom I behold as my King. I consider myself as the most wretched of men. I am full of faults, flaws, and weaknesses, and have committed all sorts of crimes against his King. Touched with a sensible regret I confess all my wickedness to Him. I ask His forgiveness. I abandon myself in His hands that He may do what He pleases with me.

My King is full of mercy and goodness. Far from chastising me, He embraces me with love. He makes me eat at His table. He serves me with His own hands and gives me the key to His treasures. He converses and delights Himself with me incessantly, in a thousand and a thousand ways. And He treats me in all respects as His favorite. In this way I consider myself continually in His holy presence.

My most usual method is this simple attention, an affectionate regard for God to whom I find myself often attached with greater sweetness and delight than that of an infant at the mother's breast. To choose an expression, I would call this state the bosom of God, for the inexpressible sweetness which I taste and experience there. If, at any time, my thoughts wander from it from necessity or infirmity, I am presently recalled by inward emotions so charming and delicious that I cannot find words to describe them. Please reflect on my great wretchedness, of which you are fully informed, rather than on the great favors God does one as unworthy and ungrateful as I am.

As for my set hours of prayer, they are simply a continuation of the same exercise. Sometimes I consider myself as a stone before a carver, whereof He is to make a statue. Presenting myself thus before God, I desire Him to make His perfect image in my soul and render me entirely like Himself. At other times, when I apply myself to prayer, I feel all my spirit lifted up without any care or effort on my part. This often continues as if it was suspended yet firmly fixed in God like a center or place of rest.

I know that some charge this state with inactivity, delusion, and self-love. I confess that it is a holy inactivity. And it would be a happy self-love if the soul, in that state, were capable of it. But while the soul is in this repose, she cannot be disturbed by the kinds of things to which she was formerly accustomed. The things that the soul used to depend on would now hinder rather than assist her.

Yet, I cannot see how this could be called imagination or delusion because the soul which enjoys God in this way wants nothing but Him. If this is delusion, then only God can remedy it. Let Him do what He pleases with me. I desire only Him and to be wholly devoted to Him.

Please send me your opinion as I greatly value and have a singular esteem for your reverence, and am yours.

Third Letter: We have a God who is infinitely gracious and knows all our wants. I always thought that He would reduce you to extremity. He will come in His own time, and when you least expect it. Hope in Him more than ever. Thank Him with me for the favors He does you, particularly for the fortitude and patience which He gives you in your afflictions. It is a plain mark of the care He takes of you. Comfort yourself with Him, and give thanks for all.

I admire also the fortitude and bravery of M—. God has given him a good disposition and a good will; but he is still a little worldly and somewhat immature. I hope the affliction God has sent him will help him do some reflection and inner searching and that it may prove to be a wholesome remedy to him. It is a chance for him to put all his trust in God who accompanies him everywhere. Let him think of Him as much as he can, especially in time of great danger.

A little lifting up of the heart and a remembrance of God suffices. One act of inward worship, though upon a march with sword in hand, are prayers which, however short, are nevertheless very acceptable to God. And, far from lessening a soldier's courage in occasions of danger, they actually serve to fortify it. Let him think of God as often as possible. Let him accustom himself, by degrees, to this small but holy exercise. No one sees it, and nothing is easier than to repeat these little internal adorations all through the day.

Please recommend to him that he think of God the most he can in this way. It is very fit and most necessary for a soldier, who is daily faced with danger to his life, and often to his very salvation.

I hope that God will assist him and all the family, to whom I present my service, being theirs and yours.

Fourth Letter: I am taking this opportunity to tell you about the sentiments of one of our society concerning the admirable effects and continual assistance he receives from the presence of God. May we both profit by them.

For the past forty years his continual care has been to be always with God; and to do nothing, say nothing, and think nothing which may displease Him. He does this without any view or motive except pure love of Him and because God deserves infinitely more.

He is now so accustomed to that Divine presence that he receives from it continual comfort and peace. For about thirty years his soul has been filled with joy and delight so continual, and sometimes so great, that he is forced to find ways to hide their appearing outwardly to others who may not understand.

If sometimes he becomes a little distracted from that Divine presence, God gently recalls Himself by a stirring in his soul. This often happens when he is most engaged in his outward chores and tasks. He answers with exact fidelity to these inward drawings, either by an elevation of his heart towards God, or by a meek and fond regard to Him, or by such words as love forms upon these occasions. For instance, he may say, "My God, here I am all devoted to You," or "Lord, make me according to Your heart."

It seems to him (in fact, he feels it) that this God of love, satisfied with such few words, reposes again and rests in the depth and center of his soul. The experience of these things gives him such certainty that God is always in the innermost part of his soul that he is beyond doubting it under any circumstances.

Judge by this what content and satisfaction he enjoys. While he continually finds within himself so great a treasure, he no longer has any need to search for it. He no longer has any anxiety about finding it because he now has his beautiful treasure open before him and may take what he pleases of it.

He often points out our blindness and exclaims that those who content themselves with so little are to be pitied. God, says he, has infinite treasure to bestow, and we take so little through routine devotion which lasts but a moment. Blind as we are, we hinder God, and stop the current of His graces. But when He finds a soul penetrated with a lively faith, He pours into it His graces and favors plentifully. There they flow like a torrent, which, after being forcibly stopped against its ordinary course, when it has found a passage, spreads itself with impetuosity and abundance.

Yet we often stop this torrent by the little value we set upon it. Let us stop it no more. Let us enter into ourselves and break down the bank which hinders it. Let us make way for grace. Let us redeem the lost time, for perhaps we have but little left. Death follows us close so let us be well prepared for it. We die but once and a mistake there is irretrievable.

I say again, let us enter into ourselves. The time presses. There is no room for delay. Our souls are at stake. It seems to me that you are prepared and have taken effectual measures so you will not be taken by surprise. I commend you for it. It is the one thing necessary. We must always work at it, because not to persevere in the spiritual life is to go back. But those who have the gale of the Holy Spirit go forward even in sleep. If the vessel of our soul is still tossed with winds and storms, let us awake the Lord who reposes in it. He will quickly calm the sea.

I have taken the liberty to impart to you these good sentiments that you may compare them with your own. May they serve to re-kindle them, if at any time they may be even a little cooled. Let us recall our first favors and remember our early joys and comforts. And, let us benefit from the example and sentiments of this brother who is little known by the world, but known and extremely caressed by God.

I will pray for you. Please pray also for me, as I am yours in our Lord.

Fifth Letter: Today I received two books and a letter from Sister M—, who is preparing to make her profession. She desires the prayers of your holy society, and yours in particular. I think she greatly values your support. Please do not disappoint her. Pray to God that she may take her vows in view of His love alone, and with a firm resolution to be wholly devoted to Him. I will send you one of those books about the presence of God; a subject which, in my opinion, contains the whole spiritual life. It seems to me that whoever duly practices it will soon become devout.

I know that for the right practice of it, the heart must be empty of all other things; because God will possess the heart alone. As He cannot possess it alone, without emptying it of all besides, so neither can He act there and do in it what He pleases unless it be left vacant to Him. There is not in the world a kind of life more sweet and delightful than that of a continual conversation with God. Only those can comprehend it who practice and experience it. Yet I do not advise you to do it from that motive. It is not pleasure which we ought to seek in this exercise. Let us do it from a principle of love, and because it is God's will for us.

Were I a preacher, I would above all other things preach the practice of the presence of God. Were I a director, I would advise all the world to do it, so necessary do I think it, and so easy too. Ah! knew we but the want we have of the grace and assistance of God, we would never lose sight of Him, no, not for a moment.

Believe me. Immediately make a holy and firm resolution never more to forget Him. Resolve to spend the rest of your days in His sacred presence, deprived of all consolations for the love of Him if He thinks fit. Set heartily about this work, and if you do it sincerely, be assured that you will soon find the effects of it.

I will assist you with my prayers, poor as they are. I recommend myself earnestly to you and those of your holy society.

Sixth Letter: I have received from M— the things which you gave her for me. I wonder that you have not given me your thoughts on the little book I sent to you and which you must have received. Set heartily about the practice of it in your old age. It is better late than never.

I cannot imagine how religious persons can live satisfied without the practice of the presence of God. For my part I keep myself retired with Him in the depth and center of my soul as much as I can. While I am with Him I fear nothing; but the least turning from Him is insupportable. This practice does not tire the body. It is, however, proper to deprive it sometimes, nay often, of many little pleasures which are innocent and lawful. God will not permit a soul that desires to be devoted entirely to Him to take pleasures other than with Him. That is more than reasonable.

I do not say we must put any violent constraint upon ourselves. No, we must serve God in a holy freedom. We must work faithfully without trouble or disquiet, recalling our mind to God mildly and with tranquillity as often as we find it wandering from Him. It is, however, necessary to put our whole trust in God. We must lay aside all other cares and even some forms of devotion, though very good in themselves, yet such as one often engages in routinely. Those devotions are only means to attain to the end. Once we have established a habit of the practice of the presence of God, we are then with Him who is our end. We have no need to return to the means. We may simply continue with Him in our commerce of love, persevering in His holy presence with an act of praise, of adoration, or of desire or with an act of resignation, or thanksgiving, and in all the ways our spirits can invent.

Be not discouraged by the repugnance which you may find in it from nature. You must sacrifice yourself. At first, one often thinks it a waste of time. But you must go on and resolve to persevere in it until death, notwithstanding all the difficulties that may occur.

I recommend myself to the prayers of your holy society, and yours in particular. I am yours in our Lord.

Seventh Letter: I pity you much. It will be a great relief if you can leave the care of your affairs to M— and spend the remainder of your life only in worshipping God. He requires no great matters of us; a little remembrance of Him from time to time, a little adoration. Sometimes to pray for His grace. Sometimes to offer Him your sufferings. And sometimes to return Him thanks for the favors He has given you, and still gives you, in the midst of your troubles. Console yourself with Him the oftenest you can. Lift up your heart to Him at your meals and when you are in company. The least little remembrance will always be pleasing to Him.

You need not cry very loud. He is nearer to us than we are aware. And we do not always have to be in church to be with God. We may make an oratory of our heart so we can, from time to time, retire to converse with Him in meekness, humility, and love. Every one is capable of such familiar conversation with God, some more, some less. He knows what we can do.

Let us begin then. Perhaps He expects but one generous resolution on our part. Have courage. We have but little time to live. You are nearly sixty-four, and I am almost eighty. Let us live and die with God.

Sufferings will be sweet and pleasant while we are with Him. Without Him, the greatest pleasures will be a cruel punishment to us. May He be blessed by all.

Gradually become accustomed to worship Him in this way; to beg His grace, to offer Him your heart from time to time; in the midst of your business, even every moment if you can. Do not always scrupulously confine yourself to certain rules or particular forms of devotion. Instead, act in faith with love and humility.

You may assure M— of my poor prayers, and that I am their servant, and yours particularly.

Eighth Letter: You tell me nothing new. You are not the only one who is troubled with wandering thoughts. Our mind is extremely roving. But the will is mistress of all our faculties. She must recall our stray thoughts and carry them to God as their final end.

If the mind is not sufficiently controlled and disciplined at our first engaging in devotion, it contracts certain bad habits of wandering and dissipation. These are difficult to overcome. The mind can draw us, even against our will, to worldly things. I believe one remedy for this is to humbly confess our faults and beg God's mercy and help.

I do not advise you to use multiplicity of words in prayer. Many words and long discourses are often the occasions of wandering. Hold yourself in prayer before God, like a dumb or paralytic beggar at a rich man's gate. Let it be your business to keep your mind in the presence of the Lord. If your mind sometimes wanders and withdraws itself from Him, do not become upset. Trouble and disquiet serve rather to distract the mind than to re-collect it. The will must bring it back in tranquillity. If you persevere in this manner, God will have pity on you.

One way to re-collect the mind easily in the time of prayer, and preserve it more in tranquillity, is not to let it wander too far at other times. Keep your mind strictly in the presence of God. Then being accustomed to think of Him often, you will find it easy to keep your mind calm in the time of prayer, or at least to recall it from its wanderings. I have told you already of the advantages we may draw from this practice of the presence of God. Let us set about it seriously and pray for one another.

Ninth Letter: The enclosed is an answer to that which I received from M—. Please deliver it to her. She is full of good will but she would go faster than grace! One does not become holy all at once. I recommend her to your guidance. We ought to help one another by our advice, and yet more by our good example. Please let me hear of her from time to time and whether she is very fervent and obedient.

Let us often consider that our only business in this life is to please God, that perhaps all besides is but folly and vanity. You and I have lived over forty years in the monastic life. Have we employed them in loving and serving God, who by His mercy has called us to this state and for that very end? I am sometimes filled with shame and confusion when I reflect, on the one hand, upon the great favors which God has done and continues to do for me; and, on the other, upon the ill use I have made of them and my small advancement in the way of perfection.

Since, by His mercy, He gives us yet a little time, let us begin in earnest. Let us repair the lost time. Let us return with full assurance to that Father of mercies, who is always ready to receive us affectionately. Let us generously renounce, for the love of Him, all that is not Himself. He deserves infinitely more. Let us think of Him perpetually. Let us put all our trust in Him.

I have no doubt that we shall soon receive an abundance of His grace, with which we can do all things, and, without which we can do nothing but sin. We cannot escape the dangers which abound in life without the actual and continual help of God. Let us pray to Him for it constantly.

How can we pray to Him without being with Him? How can we be with Him but in thinking of Him often? And how can we often think of Him, but by a holy habit which we should form of it? You will tell me that I always say the same thing. It is true, for this is the best and easiest method I know. I use no other. I advise all the world to do it.

We must know before we can love. In order to know God, we must often think of Him. And when we come to love Him, we shall then also think of Him often, for our heart will be with our treasure.

Tenth Letter: I have had a good deal of difficulty bringing myself to write to M.—. I do it now purely because you desire me to do so. Please address it and send it to him.

It is pleasing to see all the faith you have in God. May He increase it in you more and more. We cannot have too much trust in so good and faithful a Friend who will never fail us in this world nor in the next.

If M.— takes advantage of the loss he has had and puts all his confidence in God, He will soon give him another friend more powerful and more inclined to serve him. He disposes of hearts as He pleases. Perhaps M.— was too attached to him he has lost. We ought to love our friends, but without encroaching upon the love of God, which must always be first.

Please keep my recommendation in mind that you think of God often; by day, by night, in your business, and even in your diversions. He is always near you and with you. Leave Him not alone. You would think it rude to leave a friend alone who came to visit you. Why, then, must God be neglected? Do not forget Him but think on Him often. Adore Him continually. Live and die with Him. This is the glorious work of a Christian; in a word, this is our profession. If we do not know it, we must learn it.

I will endeavor to help you with my prayers, and am yours in our Lord.

Eleventh Letter: I do not pray that you may be delivered from your pains; but I pray earnestly that God gives you strength and patience to bear them as long as He pleases. Comfort yourself with Him who holds you fastened to the cross. He will loose you when He thinks fit. Happy are those who suffer with Him. Accustom yourself to suffer in that manner, and seek from Him the strength to endure as much, and as long, as He judges necessary for you.

Worldly people do not comprehend these truths. It is not surprising though, since they suffer like what they are and not like Christians. They see sickness as a pain against nature and not as a favor from God. Seeing it only in that light, they find nothing in it but grief and distress. But those who consider sickness as coming from the hand of God, out of His mercy and as the means He uses for their salvation, commonly find sweetness and consolation in it.

I pray that you see that God is often nearer to us and present within us in sickness than in health. Do not rely completely on another physician because He reserves your cure to Himself. Put all your trust in God. You will soon find the effects in your recovery, which we often delay by putting greater faith in medicine than in God.

Whatever remedies you use, they will succeed only so far as He permits. When pains come from God, only He can ultimately cure them. He often sends sickness to the body to cure diseases of the soul. Comfort yourself with the Sovereign Physician of both soul and body.

I expect you will say that I am very much at ease, and that I eat and drink at the table of the Lord. You have reason. But think how painful it would be to the greatest criminal in the world to eat at the king's table and be served by him, yet have no assurance of pardon? I believe he would feel an anxiety that nothing could calm except his trust in the goodness of his sovereign. So I assure you, that whatever pleasures I taste at the table of my King, my sins, ever present before my eyes, as well as the uncertainty of my pardon, torment me. Though I accept that torment as something pleasing to God.

Be satisfied with the condition in which God places you. However happy you may think me, I envy you. Pain and suffering would be a paradise to me, if I could suffer with my God. The greatest pleasures would be hell if I relished them without Him. My only consolation would be to suffer something for His sake.

I must, in a little time, go to God. What comforts me in this life is that I now see Him by faith. I see Him in such a manner that I sometimes say, I believe no more, but I see. I feel what faith teaches us, and, in that assurance and that practice of faith, I live and die with Him.

Stay with God always for He is the only support and comfort for your affliction. I shall beseech Him to be with you. I present my service.

Twelfth Letter: If we were well accustomed to the practice of the presence of God, bodily discomforts would be greatly alleviated. God often permits us to suffer a little to purify our souls and oblige us to stay close to Him.

Take courage. Offer Him your pain and pray to Him for strength to endure them. Above all, get in the habit of often thinking of God, and forget Him the least you can. Adore Him in your infirmities. Offer yourself to Him from time to time. And, in the height of your sufferings, humbly and affectionately beseech Him (as a child his father) to make you conformable to His holy will. I shall endeavor to assist you with my poor prayers.

God has many ways of drawing us to Himself. He sometimes seems to hide Himself from us. But faith alone ought to be our support. Faith is the foundation of our confidence. We must put all our faith in God. He will not fail us in time of need. I do not know how God will dispose of me but I am always happy. All the world suffers and I, who deserve the severest discipline, feel joys so continual and great that I can scarcely contain them.

I would willingly ask God for a part of your sufferings. I know my weakness is so great that if He left me one moment to myself, I would be the most wretched man alive. And yet, I do not know how He could leave me alone because faith gives me as strong a conviction as reason. He never forsakes us until we have first forsaken Him. Let us fear to leave Him. Let us always be with Him. Let us live and die in His presence. Do pray for me, as I pray for you.

Thirteenth Letter: I am sorry to see you suffer so long. What gives me some ease and sweetens the feeling I have about your griefs, is that they are proof of God's love for you. See your pains in that view and you will bear them more easily. In your case, it is my opinion that, at this point, you should discontinue human remedies and resign yourself entirely to the providence of God. Perhaps He waits only for that resignation and perfect faith in Him to cure you. Since, in spite of all the care you have taken, treatment has proved unsuccessful and your malady still increases, wait no longer. Put yourself entirely in His hands and expect all from Him.

I told you in my last letter that He sometimes permits bodily discomforts to cure the distempers of the soul. Have courage. Make a virtue of necessity. Do not ask God for deliverance from your pain. Instead, out of love for Him, ask for the strength to resolutely bear all that He pleases, and as long as He pleases. Such prayers are hard at first, but they are very pleasing to God, and become sweet to those that love Him.

Love sweetens pains. And when one loves God, one suffers for His sake with joy and courage. Do so, I beseech you. Comfort yourself with Him. He is the only physician for all our illnesses. He is the Father of the afflicted and always ready to help us. He loves us infinitely more than we can imagine. Love Him in return and seek no consolation elsewhere. I hope you will soon receive His comfort. Adieu.

I will help you with my prayers, poor as they are, and shall always be yours in our Lord.

Fourteenth Letter: I give thanks to our Lord for having relieved you a little as you desired. I have often been near death and I was never so much satisfied as then. At those times I did not pray for any relief, but I prayed for strength to suffer with courage, humility, and love. How sweet it is to suffer with God! However great your sufferings may be, receive them with love. It is paradise to suffer and be with Him. If, in this life, we might enjoy the peace of paradise, we must accustom ourselves to a familiar, humble, and affectionate conversation with God.

We must hinder our spirits wandering from Him on all occasions. We must make our heart a spiritual temple so we can constantly adore Him. We must continually watch over ourselves so we do not do anything that may displease Him. When our minds and hearts are filled with God, suffering becomes full of unction and consolation.

I well know that to arrive at this state, the beginning is very difficult because we must act purely on faith. But, though it is difficult, we know also that we can do all things with the grace of God. He never refuses those who ask earnestly. Knock. Persevere in knocking. And I answer for it, that, in His due time, He will open His graces to you. He will grant, all at once, what He has deferred during many years. Adieu.

Pray to Him for me, as I pray to Him for you. I hope to see Him soon.

Fifteenth Letter: God knows best what we need. All that He does is for our good. If we knew how much He loves us, we would always be ready to receive both the bitter and the sweet from His Hand. It would make no difference. All that came from Him would be pleasing. The worst afflictions only appear intolerable if we see them in the wrong light. When we see them as coming from the hand of God and know that it is our loving Father who humbles and distresses us, our sufferings lose their bitterness and can even become a source of consolation.

Let all our efforts be to know God. The more one knows Him, the greater one desires to know Him. Knowledge is commonly the measure of love. The deeper and more extensive our knowledge, the greater is our love. If our love of God were great we would love Him equally in pain and pleasure.

We only deceive ourselves by seeking or loving God for any favors which He has or may grant us. Such favors, no matter how great, can never bring us as near to God as can one simple act of faith. Let us seek Him often by faith. He is within us. Seek Him not elsewhere.

Are we not rude and deserve blame if we leave Him alone to busy ourselves with trifles which do not please Him and perhaps even offend Him? These trifles may one day cost us dearly. Let us begin earnestly to be devoted to Him. Let us cast everything else out of our hearts. He wants to possess the heart alone. Beg this favor of Him. If we do all we can, we will soon see that change wrought in us which we so greatly desire.

I cannot thank Him enough for the relief He has given you. I hope to see Him within a few days. Let us pray for one another.

Brother Lawrence died peacefully within days of this last letter.

Made in the USA
Coppell, TX
06 March 2023

13883562R00031